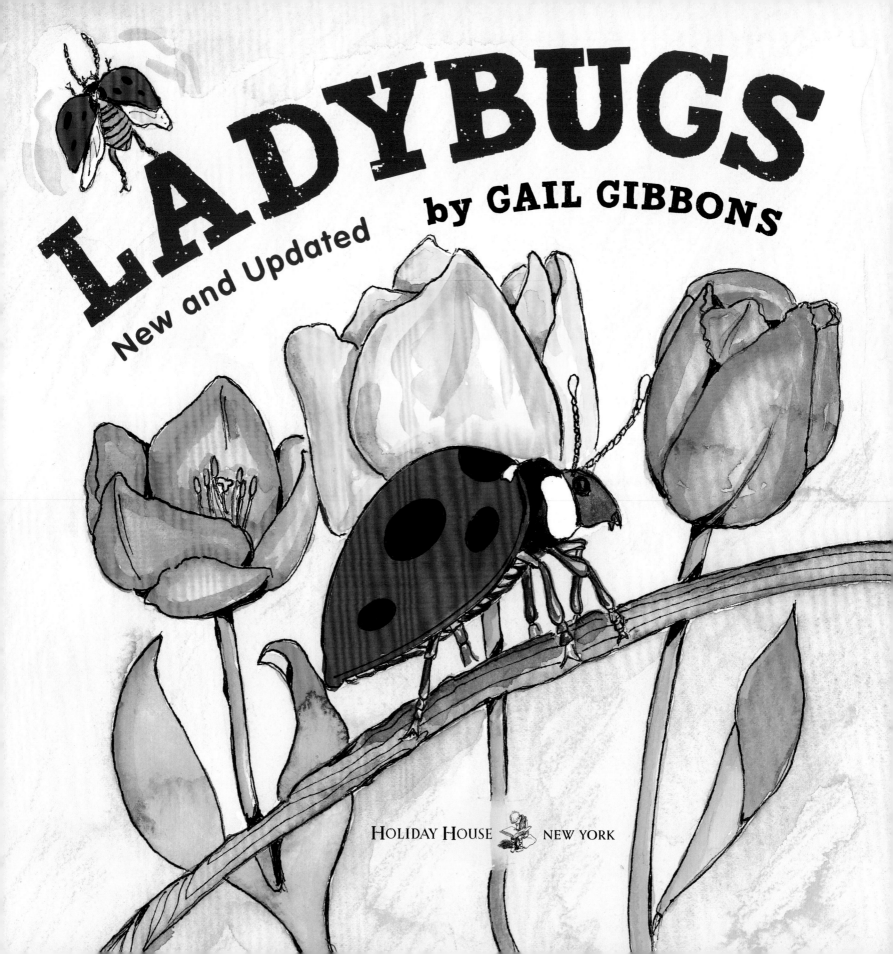

LADYBUGS

New and Updated

by GAIL GIBBONS

HOLIDAY HOUSE · NEW YORK

To Marilyn Chasan

Special thanks to Paul Johnson,
University of New Hampshire-Durham,
Department of Natural Resources
and the Environment

Special thanks to Jody Green,
Ph.D., BCE Assistant Educator,
University of Nebraska

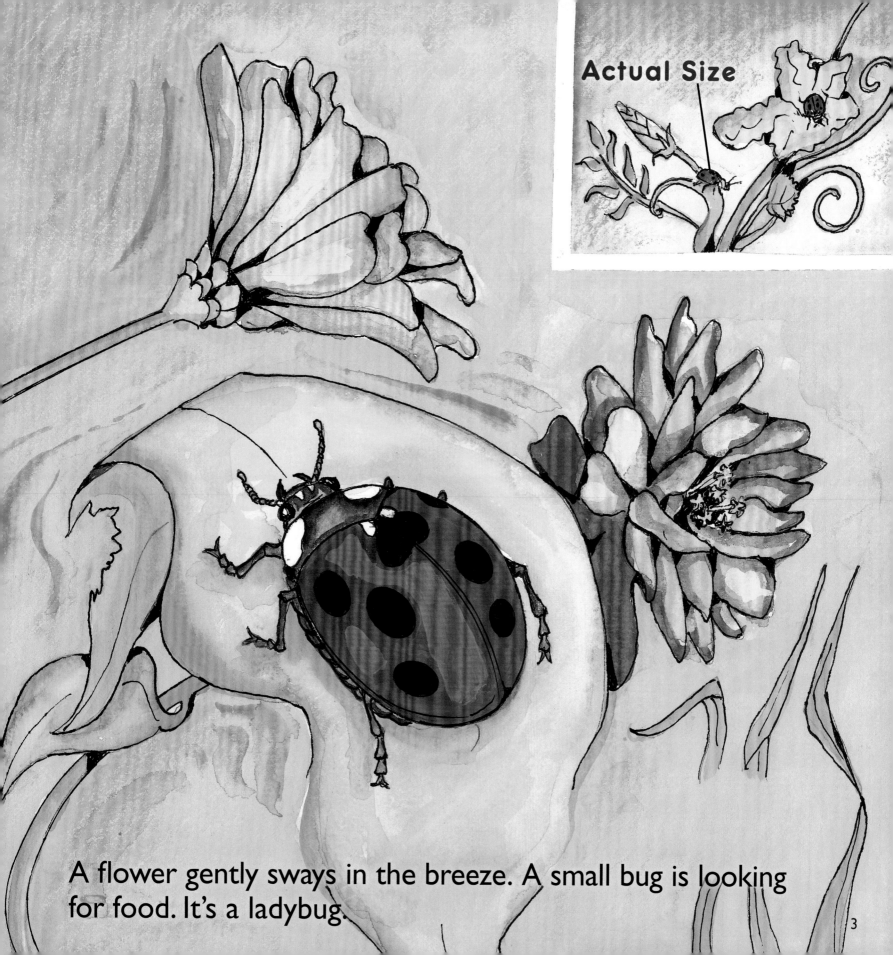

Actual Size

A flower gently sways in the breeze. A small bug is looking for food. It's a ladybug.

MITES

APHIDS

SCALES

Many ladybugs fly and move about looking for food. They eat aphids (AA-fidz) and other insects such as scales and mites that are harmful to plants.

A BEETLE is an insect with a hard outside covering and two pairs of wings.

A ladybug is a beetle. The hard outside of an adult ladybug's body protects its soft insides and wings.

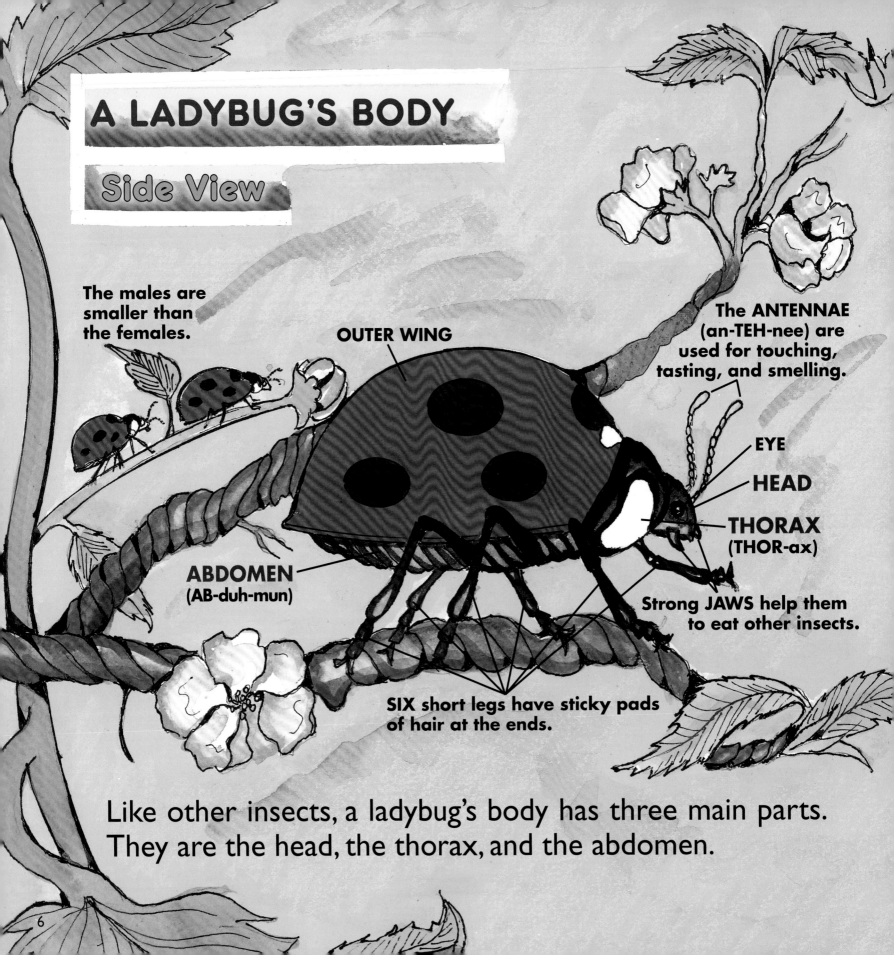

A LADYBUG'S BODY

Side View

The males are smaller than the females.

OUTER WING

The ANTENNAE (an-TEH-nee) are used for touching, tasting, and smelling.

EYE

HEAD

THORAX (THOR-ax)

Strong JAWS help them to eat other insects.

ABDOMEN (AB-duh-mun)

SIX short legs have sticky pads of hair at the ends.

Like other insects, a ladybug's body has three main parts. They are the head, the thorax, and the abdomen.

OUTER WINGS are hard and protect the inner wings.

THORAX

INNER WINGS are delicate and are used for flying.

The ladybug has two sets of wings.

DIFFERENT KINDS OF LADYBUGS

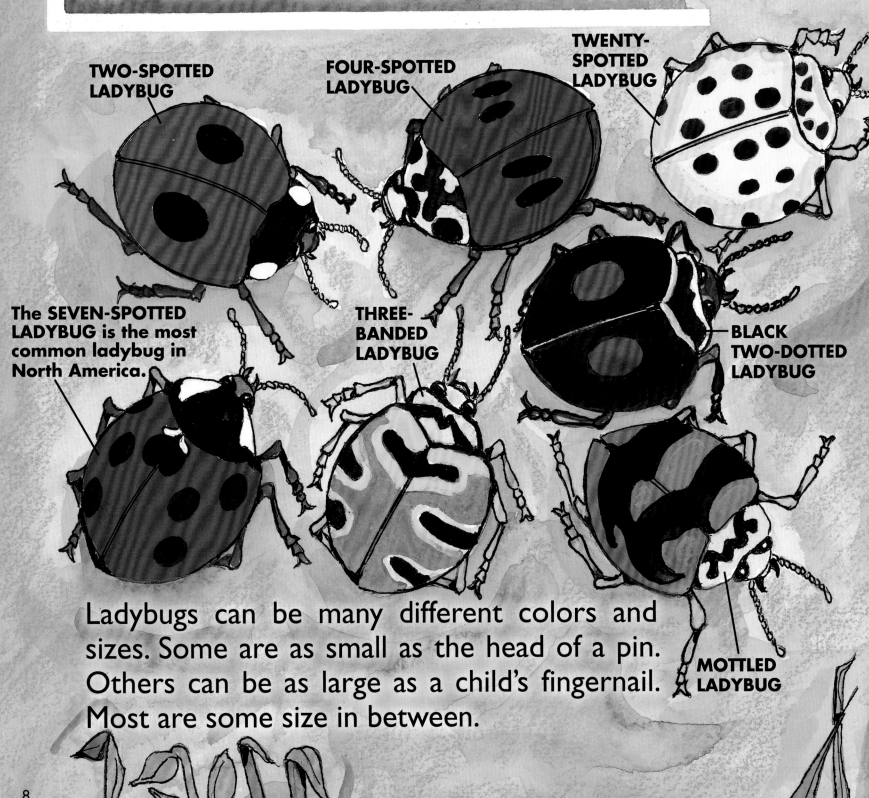

TWO-SPOTTED LADYBUG

FOUR-SPOTTED LADYBUG

TWENTY-SPOTTED LADYBUG

The SEVEN-SPOTTED LADYBUG is the most common ladybug in North America.

THREE-BANDED LADYBUG

BLACK TWO-DOTTED LADYBUG

MOTTLED LADYBUG

Ladybugs can be many different colors and sizes. Some are as small as the head of a pin. Others can be as large as a child's fingernail. Most are some size in between.

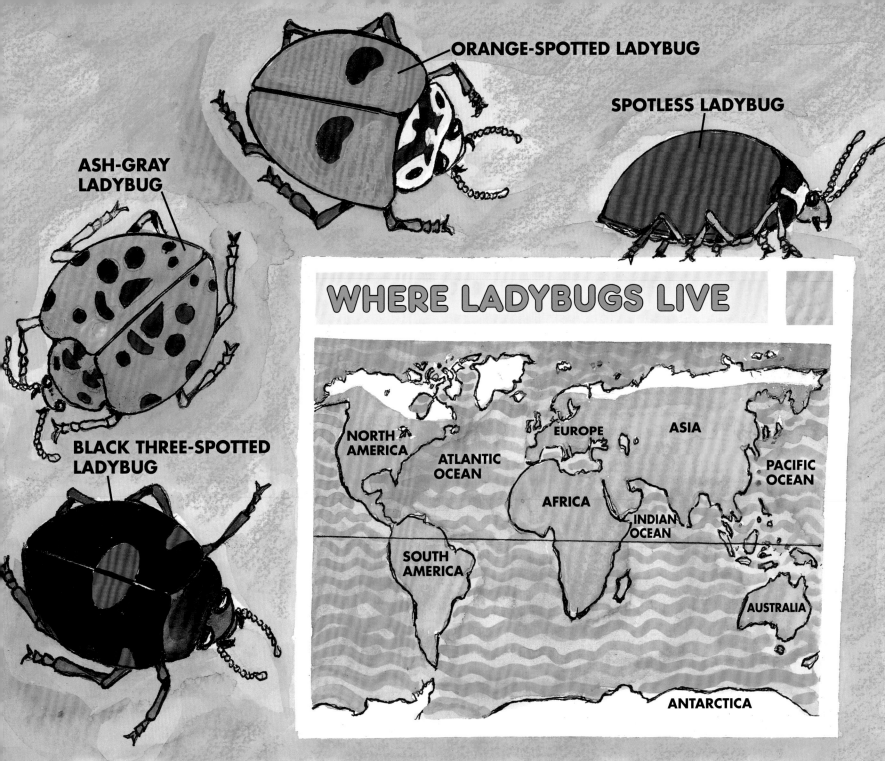

ORANGE-SPOTTED LADYBUG

SPOTLESS LADYBUG

ASH-GRAY LADYBUG

BLACK THREE-SPOTTED LADYBUG

WHERE LADYBUGS LIVE

NORTH AMERICA

EUROPE

ASIA

ATLANTIC OCEAN

PACIFIC OCEAN

AFRICA

INDIAN OCEAN

SOUTH AMERICA

AUSTRALIA

ANTARCTICA

They live on six of the seven continents. Many scientists believe there are about 6,000 different kinds of ladybugs around the world. They also believe there are about 475 different types of ladybugs in North America.

THE FOUR STAGES—FROM EGG TO ADULT LADYBUG

FIRST STAGE

Eggs

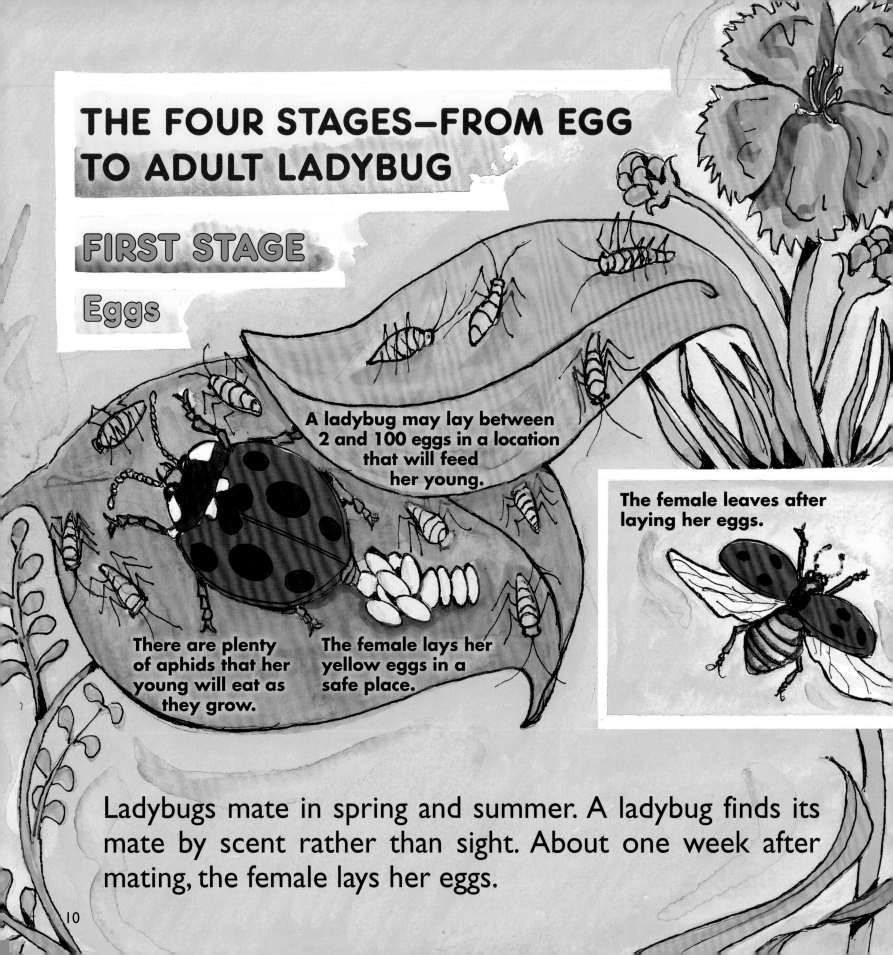

A ladybug may lay between 2 and 100 eggs in a location that will feed her young.

There are plenty of aphids that her young will eat as they grow.

The female lays her yellow eggs in a safe place.

The female leaves after laying her eggs.

Ladybugs mate in spring and summer. A ladybug finds its mate by scent rather than sight. About one week after mating, the female lays her eggs.

During the next week the eggs turn from yellow to green or gray.

SECOND STAGE
Larvae

After a few days, the eggs are ready to hatch. The thin shells begin to split open. The ladybug larvae (LAR-vee) crawl out. They eat their eggshells and begin eating aphids.

OLD OUTSIDE COVERING

One larva (LAR-vuh) can eat about thirty aphids a day. A larva eats so much that its outside covering becomes too tight. The outside covering splits and is shed. A new larger outside covering takes its place. This is called molting.

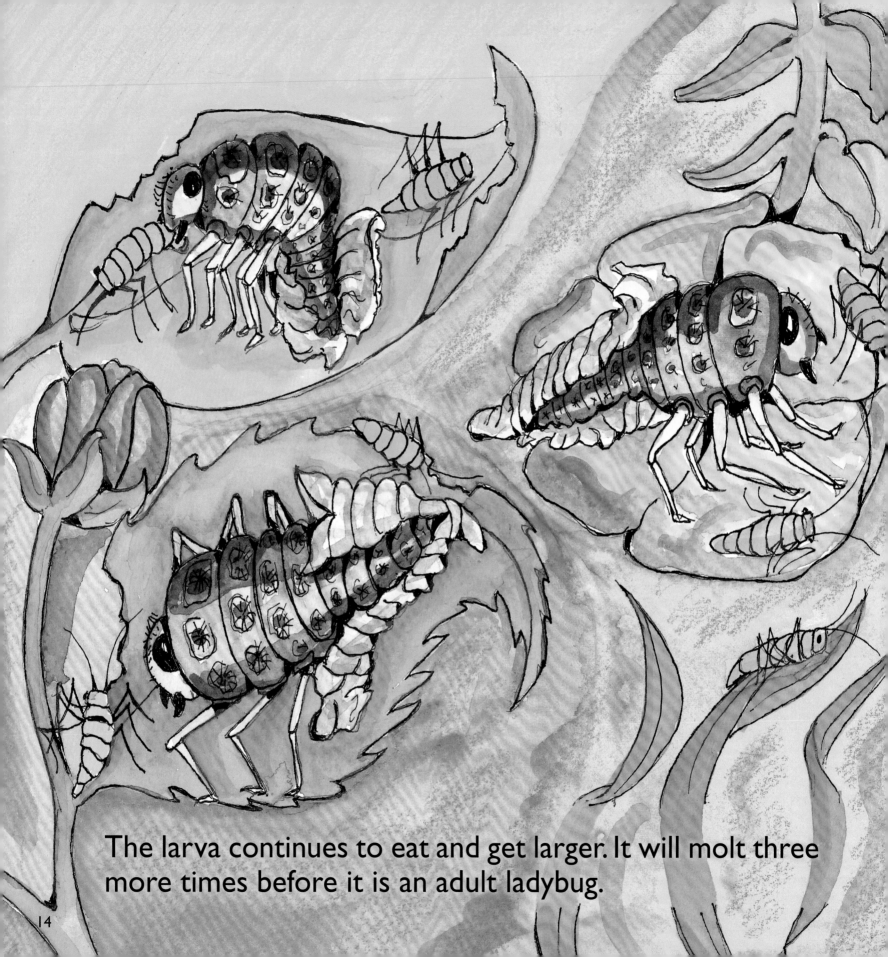

The larva continues to eat and get larger. It will molt three more times before it is an adult ladybug.

After molting for the last time, the larva attaches itself to a safe place using a sticky liquid at the end of its abdomen.

Pupa

The ladybug larva is now called a pupa (PEW-puh). Outside, the covering of the pupa is becoming hard.

Inside, the ladybug pupa will continue to develop. It will not eat or move during this time.

Now the ladybug pupa begins to split open its hard covering. Headfirst, the ladybug pulls its body out. The ladybug's body is pale and soft, and has no dots.

18

INNER WINGS

OUTER WINGS

Its body slowly hardens. Its two delicate transparent inner wings, which will be used for flying, extend to dry. Then they slip back under the hard outer wings for protection.

Ladybugs crawl around
more than they fly.

In about one hour the ladybug is ready to live a ladybug's life. Dots begin to appear.

Soon the adult ladybug opens its hard wings and unfolds its flying wings. The ladybug lifts itself up in the air. It will spend its life going from plant to plant eating aphids and other insects.

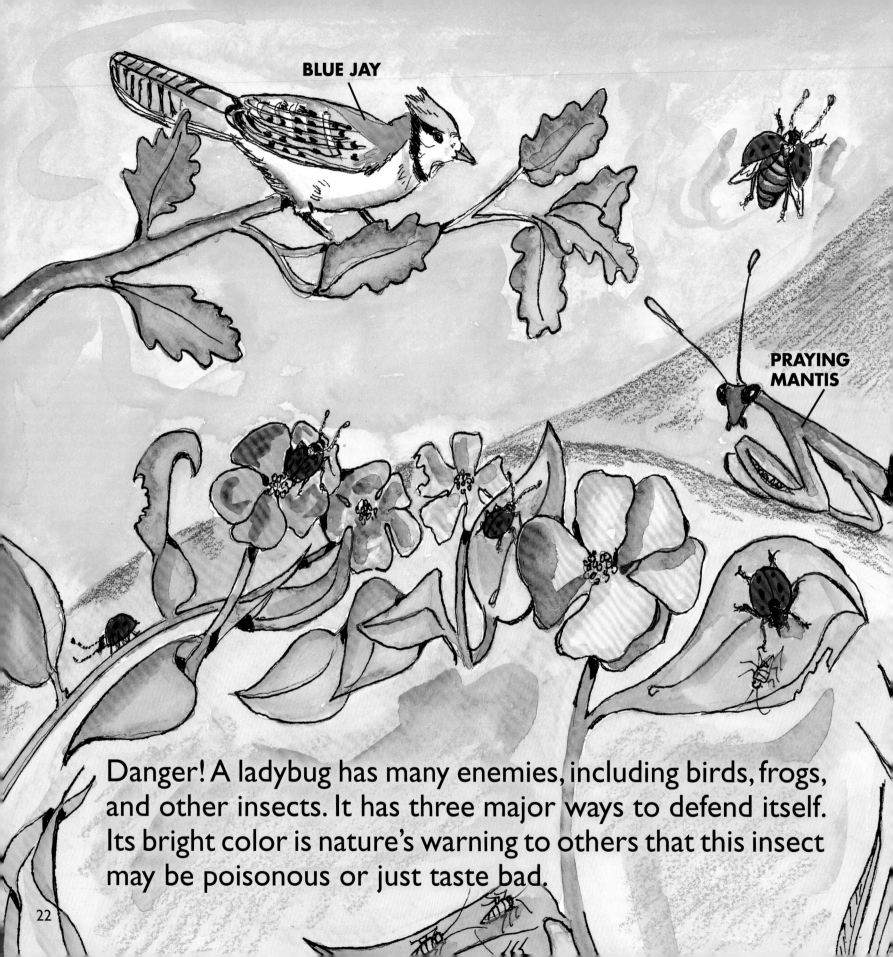

BLUE JAY

PRAYING MANTIS

Danger! A ladybug has many enemies, including birds, frogs, and other insects. It has three major ways to defend itself. Its bright color is nature's warning to others that this insect may be poisonous or just taste bad.

LEOPARD
FROG

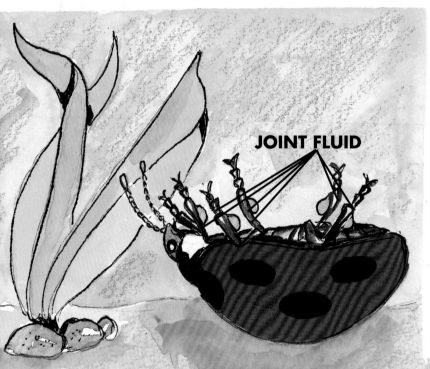

JOINT FLUID

When a ladybug is attacked, its leg joints ooze a yellow fluid. It
has a terrible smell that keeps enemies away. A ladybug will also
pretend to be dead, and then the predator will lose interest.

Some ladybugs fly to a warmer climate.

Ladybugs must protect themselves from cold winter weather. Thousands of ladybugs find a safe, warm place such as under a rock or nestled under leaves.

Like other insects, ladybugs are cold-blooded. Their body temperatures are controlled by the air surrounding them. They become active again when the outside temperature rises above 55° Fahrenheit (13° Celsius) or to about 56° Fahrenheit (13.3° Celsius).

Gardeners and farmers have always been against insects that damage their plants and crops, but they appreciate ladybugs because they eat plant-damaging insects.

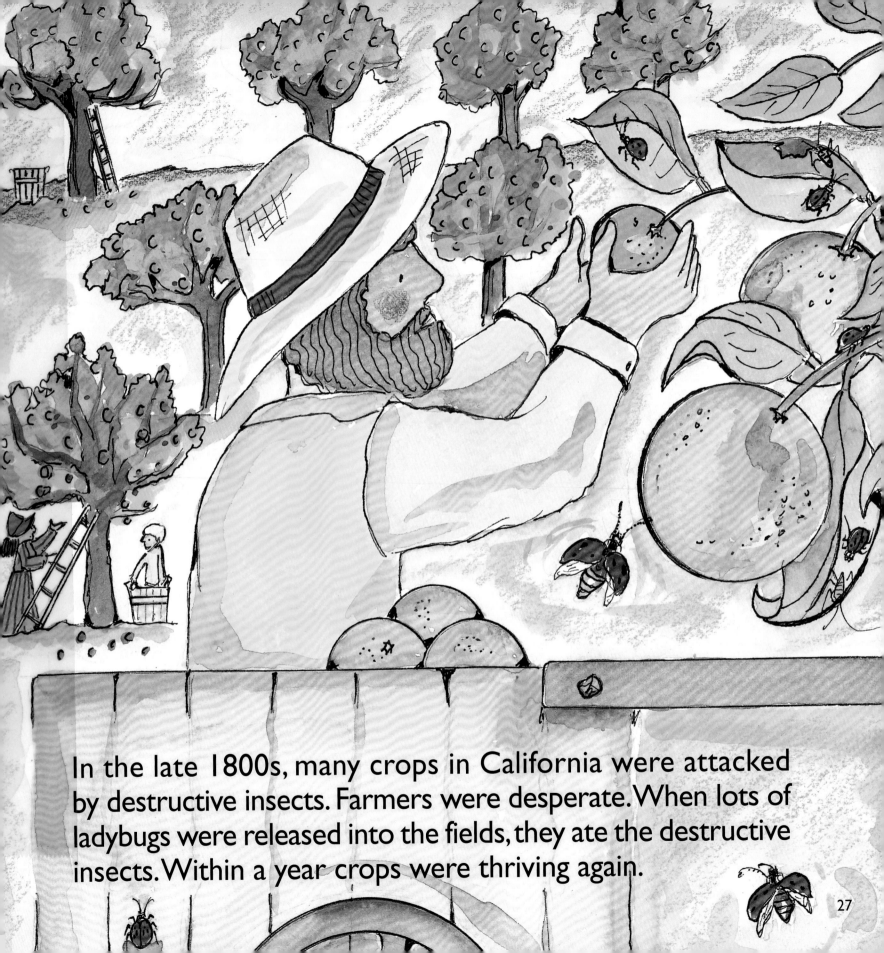

In the late 1800s, many crops in California were attacked by destructive insects. Farmers were desperate. When lots of ladybugs were released into the fields, they ate the destructive insects. Within a year crops were thriving again.

PESTICIDES are chemicals sprayed on crops to kill insects.

When farms became larger, farmers began to use poisonous pesticides to kill plant-eating insects. With time, some farmers realized that those pesticides could be bad for the crops because they damaged soil, polluted water, and were harmful to wildlife, including ladybugs.

Today, agriculture experts are finding safer ways to protect crops, which include using ladybugs again.

Organic foods are grown without using chemicals. Many plants have ladybugs helping them to become insect-free and grow into delicious foods that we can eat.

Ladybugs are beautiful to look at and interesting to watch, but they are also important insects that help the environment.

LADYBUGS. . .

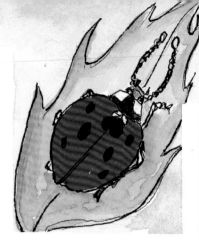

It takes thousands of ladybugs to protect 1 acre (4,046.8 square meters) of plants.

Ladybugs are also called lady beetles, ladybirds, or ladybird beetles.

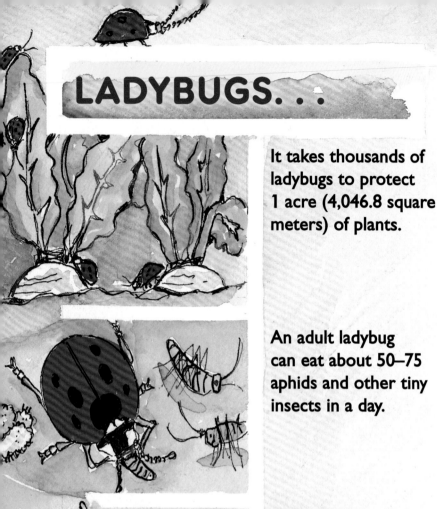

An adult ladybug can eat about 50–75 aphids and other tiny insects in a day.

Ladybugs can float on water and paddle.

A ladybug's inner wings beat 85 times per second.

Some ladybugs have no dots or patterns.

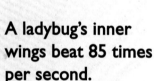

Depending on the kind of ladybug, some can live for about a month while others can live to be 2 years old.

Ladybugs can fly about 18 miles (30 kilometers) per hour.

WEBSITES

In the United States:
https://www.nationalgeographic.com/animals/invertebrates/facts/ladybugs

In Canada:
canadiangeographic.ca/kids/animal-facts/lady_bug.asp